Lake Tahoe

The Andersen's 1996
Hope you enjoy
these beautiful pictures
of your new home
at Lake Tahoe

Georgia McBryan

An aerial view of
sandy, shallow lake
bottom falling away
into the deep, blue
depths. Overleaf:
Sunrise seen from the
top of Rubicon Peak
looking down on
Rubicon Bay. Cover:
One of Nature's finest
works, Emerald Bay is
set aglow by the
colors of dawn.

Lake Tahoe

A Photo Essay of

the Lake Tahoe Region

by Larry Prosor

Text by

Leo Poppoff

Fine Line Productions

To Mother Nature.

For every book sold, a contribution will be made to the Preserve Lake Tahoe Fund, a non-profit fund set up to help in the battle to maintain Lake Tahoe's unique clarity and purity.

Photos © Larry Prosor 1988
Text © Leo Poppoff 1988
ISBN #0-9620148-0-X

Published by: Fine Line Productions
    P.O. Box 2452
    Truckee, California 95734
    916/587-0760
Produced by: Larry Prosor and David Zischke
Design and Layout: Foley and Associates
Text Editor: Laurel Hilde Lippert
Photo Editors: Susan Foley, Larry Prosor and David Zischke
Captions: Larry Prosor
Printed by Dai Nippon/Japan

For information regarding use or purchase of individual photos in this book, please contact:
    INSTOCK, Inc.
    P.O. Box 2668
    Truckee, California 95734
    916/587-7989

Special thanks to these people who were helpful in creating this book:

Ace Anderson	Whitney Prosor
Chris Delumyea	Rick Reynolds
Raymond DeVre	Lee Schmidt
Eric Efthimou	Scot Schmidt
Kathy Gelso	Ray Shady
Jeff Hartley	Larry Sherman
Rob Huntoon	Natalie Snider
Ruthann Lo	Debbie Thomas
Mr. & Mrs. William L. Martin	Peter Underwood
Kirby Moulton	Jimmy Vaughn
Chris Paragay	Steve Wandt
Nadine Powers	Mr. & Mrs. James B. Zischke
Cindy Prosor	

And to these companies and ski areas that gave their assistance:

Alpine Meadows	Salomon/ North America
Canon USA	
Fischer of America	Skis Dynastar
Mt. Rose/ Slide Mountain	Sugar Bowl
The North Face	Tahoe Donner Cross Country
Royal Gorge	

Contents

THE FINAL COLORS OF
DAYLIGHT.

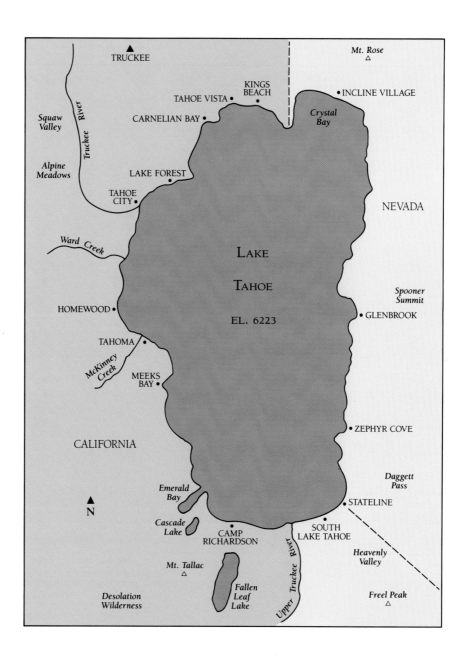

TRUCKEE

Squaw
Valley

Truckee River

Alpine
Meadows

CARNELIAN BAY •

TAHOE VISTA •

KINGS
BEACH

• INCLINE VILLAGE

Mt. Rose
△

Crystal
Bay

LAKE FOREST

TAHOE
CITY •

NEVADA

Ward Creek

LAKE

TAHOE

EL. 6223

Spooner
Summit

HOMEWOOD •

• GLENBROOK

TAHOMA •

McKinney Creek

MEEKS
BAY •

• ZEPHYR COVE

CALIFORNIA

Daggett
Pass

Emerald
Bay

▲
N

Cascade
Lake

CAMP
RICHARDSON

• STATELINE

SOUTH
LAKE TAHOE

Heavenly
Valley

Mt. Tallac
△

Upper Truckee River

Desolation
Wilderness

Fallen
Leaf
Lake

Freel Peak
△

OVERLEAF: LATE

AFTERNOON THUNDER

SHOWERS POUR DOWN

UPON SAILBOATS

SILHOUETTED AGAINST A

MOUNTAINOUS BACKDROP.

Magic Leaves and Melting Snows

BY LEO POPPOFF

On one of those breathtaking, bitter cold days in the Sierra Nevada, a group of explorers slogged through deep snow drifts, struggling to cross an uncharted central Sierra pass. Often, they were forced to make wide detours to find exposed rock ridges in order to progress and conserve strength. Circling the explorers, skimming the snow like birds, were Indians on snow shoes, warmly robed in rabbit furs; they laughed at the white man's struggles, but wisely stayed out of reach.

The party was under the command of Captain John Charles Fremont and included the legendary guide Christopher "Kit" Carson and topographer Charles Preuss. They were surveying a new route to California, then under the control of Mexico. The Indians were a group of Washo from the area now known as Woodfords in Alpine County; later, they shared their precious stock of pinenut flour with the explorers and guided them over the pass.

On St. Valentine's day, February 14, 1844, near the top of what we now call Carson Pass, the explorers stopped to rest and reconnoiter. Some 16 miles to the north, they saw an impressive large lake, nestled between two mountain ranges. Preuss labeled it "Mountain Lake" on his map. Fremont insisted on calling it "Lake Bonpland," after the eminent French botanist and explorer, Aime' Jacques Alexandre Bonpland. That was the first recorded sighting, by a white person, of the national treasure that we now call "Lake Tahoe."

The official name adopted a few years later by the State of California was "Lake Bigler," after Governor "Honest John" Bigler, who had personally led a rescue party into Lake Valley (at the southern end of the Tahoe basin) during the winter of 1852. After Bigler fell out of favor, because of his leanings toward the Confederacy during the Civil War, many other names were used unofficially: Big Truckee Lake, Sierra Lake, Lake Te-ho, Maheon Lake.

The name that finally stuck, though not without controversy between California and Nevada, was Tahoe. It's commonly believed that Tahoe is an Indian word for "Big Waters." Washo history explains it differently: Washo summer camps were on the *Da ow·a ga*, which means "edge of the lake." It seems that white people mispronounced *Da ow* as Tahoe. Mark Twain insisted that the Indians were playing a joke on gullible whites; he wrote that Tahoe really meant grasshopper soup.

Bureaucracy being what it is, it took 75 years for California to recognize the name Tahoe as official. The name Lake Bigler was rescinded by the California legislature on July 18, 1945.

The Lake Tahoe basin "discovered" by Fremont's party was temporarily uninhabited. Its regular denizens, the Washo, were wintering in the Washoe and Carson Valleys a few miles to the east. They were struggling to survive until the snows melted and they could return to the cornucopia at the lake.

For several thousand years, the Washo inhabited the region from Honey Lake Valley in Lassen County south to Woodfords in Alpine County. Lake Tahoe, in the midst of this territory, was the cultural and spiritual hub of Washo life. The lake and the surrounding basin supplied much of their food and fiber.

The Washo had been in the area so long their legends didn't deal with migration to the area; it was assumed that their ancestors were created in the Tahoe basin. Their many legends covered monsters in the lake, water babies, and spirits. And, of course, they told how Lake Tahoe was formed.

According to one Washo story, a brave was fleeing one of those legendary evil spirits. A good spirit gave the Indian a handful of magic leaves. Where the leaves were cast on the ground, water appeared; fortunately, the evil spirit couldn't cross water. The brave threw down a branch full of leaves, and a huge lake (Tahoe) grew. But the evil spirit was determined and ran around the lake to continue the chase. The brave ran west out of the basin, throwing leaves as he went to slow down the evil one. Lakes sprouted from each leaf, and formed a chain into Desolation Valley and up to Echo Summit. Of course, one of those lakes is known today as Fallen Leaf Lake.

Other legends described the formation of the lake in other creative ways. But white man, not nearly as romantic as the Washo, has a different story.

According to white man's legend, based on geological observations, the Tahoe basin was formed during several very violent periods—more than a million generations ago. An ancient sea bed, covered and mixed with granitic intrusions, buckled and cracked to form a mountain range. During this turmoil (which took several million years), part of the mountain range split in three. The middle block dropped to form a steep-sided canyon, while the surrounding blocks rose to form the Sierra escarpment to the west and the Carson Range to the east.

Years later, perhaps 100,000 generations ago, volcanic flows plugged the north end of the basin, creating a natural dam.

This same process formed the many ranges and basins that characterize the landscape between the Sierra in California and the Wasatch Range in Utah. But a unique combination of climatic and geologic processes transformed the Tahoe basin into a sub-alpine marvel, quite unlike its sister basins in the deserts to the east.

Sopping wet air flows from the Pacific Ocean and tries to cross the country. When wet air masses hit the Sierra Nevada range, they must rise; to do that, air masses must drop their load of water. In winter, that load covers the Sierra with a thick mantle of snow. The winter snowpack provides water for California and western Nevada during normally dry summers. Because those air masses lose most of their water cargo in the struggle to cross the Sierra, little water is left for Nevada.

After its formation, winter rains and snow easily filled the basin. At present, the lake has a maximum depth of 1,645 feet and an average depth of 1,000 feet. Tahoe is shaped like an oval roughly 12 miles wide and 22 miles long, with a surface area of 122,000 acres.

The lake holds more than 40 trillion gallons; that's enough water to cover all of California to a depth of 14 inches, but it would only be enough to supply the state's needs for about three and a half years. More than three feet of water evaporates from the lake each year; that's some 120 billion gallons, or enough to supply nearly a half million households. It's estimated that it would take some 700 years to fill the basin with current rainfalls.

Nowadays, snowpacks melt during the summer. Water flows to Lake Tahoe and spills out to the Truckee River which flows to Pyramid Lake, northeast of Reno. But during five separate periods in Tahoe's history, summers were too cold for mountain snowpacks to melt.

Snow accumulated year after year during those glacial periods; it fell faster in winter than summer melting could remove it. The pressure of accumulating snow compressed lower layers to produce icy glaciers, perhaps a thousand feet thick. The western side of the lake was covered with ice from the mountain tops down to the lake. On the drier eastern range, glaciers developed only in shaded canyons at higher altitudes.

The tremendous pressure of the ice pushed glaciers down the valleys into the lake, scouring rock as they went. Rocks pushed ahead of the glacier formed moraines that dammed water as glaciers melted and receded. Melting glacier water carried sediments which were deposited in deltas or outwashes.

Lake Valley, at the south end of the Tahoe basin, and the lower reaches of the Upper Truckee and Trout creeks are good examples of glacial outwash. Huge underground aquifers were formed by glacial deposits on the southern and western slopes of the Tahoe basin. Emerald Bay, Cascade and Fallen Leaf Lakes were scooped out by glaciers and dammed by residual moraines.

Ice repeatedly blocked the basin's outlet, raising the lake level 600 to 800 feet higher than we see it today. When those ice dams were breached, unimaginable floods carried granite boulders down the Truckee River and rolled them beyond Reno.

There seems to be evidence that the Washo people met white people, probably Spanish explorers and American mountain men, before they encountered the Fremont party in 1844. There's no evidence, however, that white men had visited the Tahoe basin during that

EMERALD BAY AND CASCADE LAKE WERE SCULPTED BY POWERFUL GLACIERS AGES AGO. LEFT: ACCORDING TO INDIAN LEGEND, MAGIC LEAVES CREATED SMALL LAKES SUCH AS THESE IN DESOLATION VALLEY.

period. Washo had the lake to themselves, with occasional intrusions by the Paiutes from the east and California tribes from the west.

When the Washo finished their summers of fishing, hunting, weaving baskets, and gathering berries and bulbs, they left virtually no sign of their activities. But within a decade of Fremont's discovery of Lake Tahoe, hordes of immigrants from the eastern United States poured through Washo lands, shoved the generous and peaceful natives aside, and altered the landscape and ecology.

Early immigrant routes to California avoided the Tahoe basin, and the few adventurers that wandered near the lake probably didn't see many of the shy Washo. In 1848, John C. "Cockeye" Johnson explored the southern end of the lake. The first settler, Martin Smith, arrived in 1851. By 1852, the first immigrant traffic crossed near the southern shore of Lake Tahoe, and the oldest Tahoe businesses, hotels and restaurants, were established.

But then, in 1859, silver was discovered in Nevada's mountains to the east of Tahoe, and a reverse migration began, from California east to the Comstock Lode and Virginia City. The main route between San Francisco and the Comstock traversed the southern part of the basin; Pioneer Trail became the route for mass migrations of people, animals, conveyances of all kinds—and the Pony Express.

In 1861, a road was established over Daggett Pass (now Kingsbury Grade) which soon became the great bonanza road to the Washoe diggings, as the Comstock and other nearby gold and silver strikes were called. By the 1860s, more than 100 waystations could be found along Pioneer Trail. By 1869, the road over Daggett Pass was considered the finest highway in the nation.

The success of the Comstock mines led to the demise of most of Tahoe's forests. Timbers were required to shore up the impressive tunnels under Virginia City; cordwood was needed to fuel steam engines. Lumber was the new bonanza, and the new rich were lumbermen.

Mark Twain hoped to make his fortune as a timber baron in 1861. Twain and a partner walked from Carson City over the mountain and down into the basin. He declared the view of the Tahoe basin to be ". . . the fairest picture the whole earth affords." He remarked on the clarity of the lake and the healthful climate. Letters showed that Twain always wanted to return to Tahoe to live. But during that summer of 1861, Twain's campfire set his lumber claim ablaze, and ended his dreams of glory.

Duane L. Bliss, who came over the hill from Carson City a decade later, knew how to organize the lumbering of the Tahoe basin. Together with D.O. Mills, a banker, and H.M. Yerington, superintendent of the Virginia and Truckee Railroad, Bliss formed the Carson-Tahoe Lumber and Fluming Company.

Logs cut from Tahoe's hillsides were milled at Glenbrook Bay on the southeast shore, hauled up the hill to Spooner Summit and flumed down to the Carson Valley. By 1875, the volume of timber from the company's Glenbrook mills was so great, a railroad was built to move lumber up to the summit. By 1891, five mills were operating at Glenbrook Bay. At the peak of the Bliss lumbering activity, 51 million board feet were cut in one season from the hillsides near Glenbrook; in addition, 32,000 cords were rafted to the mills from the southern and western shores.

Other lumber operators, such as Walter S. Hobart, worked over the north and west shores of the lake and helped to swell the flood of timber flowing from the Tahoe basin. An estimated 72 million board feet of lumber was shipped to the Comstock mines during their busiest year. Before the tree-chopping frenzy ended, some 70 percent of the basin had been clear cut. Much of the watershed resembled abandoned battlefields.

Today, lush second growth timber masks logging scars. Glenbrook Inn and a collection of rotting pilings in Glenbrook Bay are all that remain from that bustling period.

Forty trillion gallons of pure mountain water is an overwhelming temptation in the arid west. Plans to harvest Tahoe's water hatched soon after the basin was settled. One of the basin's early water entrepreneurs was Colonel Alexis Waldemar Von Schmidt. In 1865, he incorporated the Lake Tahoe and San Francisco Water Company. His plan was to divert the Truckee River to a tunnel under Donner Summit and from there to San Francisco and farms along the way. Schmidt managed to build an impoundment dam near the lake's outlet at Tahoe City and a diversion dam a few miles downstream, but the enterprise failed. Eventually, Schmidt's Tahoe City dam was taken over by the Donner Lumber and Boom Company and used to impound water needed to flush logs down the river.

WATER FROM THE MELTING SNOWS ON MT. TALLAC HELPS BRING SNOW LAKE INTO EXISTENCE. LEFT: TAHOE'S FORESTS ARE NEARLY HEALED AFTER YEARS OF ABUSE FROM LOGGING.

Nevadans early recognized the value of Tahoe's water. Fate may have placed the outlet of the lake in California, but Nevadans believe the water was put there for Nevada's use. One of the reasons for setting aside federal forest reserves in the Tahoe basin was to preserve the remaining watershed and guarantee a water supply for Nevada's power and irrigation.

In 1903, the Federal Reclamation Service (now Bureau of Reclamation) was created by President Theodore Roosevelt. Their first project was to reclaim desert lands around Fallon, Nevada, using water from the Truckee and Carson Rivers for irrigation. It wasn't long before they needed more water and proceeded to take over the Tahoe City Dam and reconstruct it.

Today, the top six feet of the lake is used as a reservoir. The reservoir is controlled by a federal watermaster who is responsible for preserving water supplies and maintaining maximum and minimum flows in the Truckee River. The watermaster is an employee of the Federal Court in Reno and carries out his duties as prescribed in a number of court orders, allocating legal uses of water from Lake Tahoe, the Truckee River, and the other reservoirs in the Truckee River drainage.

On its way down the Truckee River to its natural sink in Pyramid Lake northeast of Reno, some of Tahoe's water is diverted over to the Lahontan Reservoir which is also the terminus of the Carson River. Water from Lahontan Reservoir is used to irrigate farms near Fallon.

Only a small amount of Lake Tahoe water is used by Tahoe basin or Truckee residents. Tahoe water, flowing down the Truckee River, supplies most of the domestic and industrial needs for Reno and Sparks. Together with Carson River water, Truckee River water is used for agricultural purposes by the Truckee-Carson Irrigation District. Each drop is precious to the burgeoning population of Reno and the harried farmers to the east.

Paiute Indians, whose tribal reservation includes Pyramid Lake, contest the current water allocations; their lake's level has dropped some 80 feet since the diversions started in 1904. In 1985, after a 12-year court battle, the Paiute tribe obtained additional spring flows of cold water to preserve their historic Lahontan cutthroat trout and the Cui-ui fisheries.

The Lahontan cutthroat trout is unique to the Tahoe-Truckee-Pyramid water system, and to Walker Lake. It's believed that the cutthroats migrated from the Columbia River system through interconnected prehistoric lakes, until they found a home in ancient Lake Lahontan. Lake Lahontan once covered nearly 9,000 square miles of Nevada and parts of California. Pyramid and Walker Lakes are the only remnants of the ancient lake.

When early white residents of Lake Tahoe and the Truckee River basins discovered the bonanza of fish in the region, they went wild. By the end of the 19th century, commercial fishermen were shipping as much as 100,000 pounds of trout each year from the Tahoe City Express office. Tahoe cutthroat trout were served in posh restaurants in San Francisco, Chicago and New Orleans. Sportsmen set records of several hundred fish caught per day per angler.

Not satisfied with the enormous harvest of cutthroats, fishery managers from Nevada and California introduced the Great Lakes mackinaw trout. The theory was that cutthroats used only the edges of the lake, so the big mackinaw could coexist by using the middle and the depths of the lake. The result would be a greatly enhanced fishery.

Over the objections of many Tahoe resort owners, mackinaw were planted in Tahoe and other lakes in the basin sometime in the latter 1800s, the exact dates are not certain.

Immigrants who remembered the wonderful little eastern "brookies" decided that they would import them to Tahoe's streams. Sportsmen packed containers full of eastern brook trout into every stream in the basin.

By the 1920s, the new fishes were well established, crowding the native cutthroats out of the way. One summer in the thirties, anglers realized that the cutthroat was gone. It's not known if the cutthroat's demise was due to fishing pressure, competition by mackinaw and brook trout, diseases introduced along with the new fishes, or the many dams that cut off their historic migrations. Fisheries managers tried to replant cutthroats and dozens of other species, but voracious mackinaw had the newcomers for lunch.

Currently, the big game fish in Lake Tahoe are these mackinaw, who grow to lengths in excess of 25 inches. There are also wild rainbow and brown trout. Fish and game authorities plant "catchable" sized rainbows every summer. Brook trout, rainbows and browns can also be caught in the basin's tributaries. Anglers must go to Pyramid Lake to find what's left of the

A LONE SAILBOAT RACES
WITH THE LAST RAYS
OF SUN.

fabulous Lahontan cutthroats.

By the end of the 19th century, the Comstock Lode had petered out and Tahoe's lumbering industry had wound down. Lumbering equipment, hotels, and waystations along the South Shore of the lake were abandoned. At the same time, the Central Pacific Railroad was providing reliable passenger service to Truckee. Travelers could take a horse-drawn stage from Truckee to Tahoe City on the North Shore. From there, steamships, such as the Governor Stanford, carried vacationers to resorts around the lake.

Bliss and his family saw the potential for tourism on the North Shore. They closed the mills at Glenbrook, loaded their railroad and shops and employees' homes on barges and moved to Tahoe City. Some of those little houses, greatly remodeled, still exist.

By 1900, the Lake Tahoe Railway and Transportation Company, with two steam engines, four passenger coaches, several box cars and 60 or 70 logging flat cars, started service between Truckee and Tahoe City. Along with the railroad, the Bliss family built the fabled Tahoe Tavern, a monument of rustic elegance, and a large beautiful steamship, S.S. Tahoe, to carry tourists to other destinations around the lake.

In the thirties, it was possible for San Franciscans to board a train in the Bay Area in the evening, and wake up the next morning on the pier next to the Tahoe Tavern and the S.S. Tahoe; all for $9.75 roundtrip. They could either stay at the posh Tavern or board the luxurious

steamship and cruise to some other resort of their choice.

Well-heeled tourists might have chosen the equally elegant Tallac House, a hotel and casino built and owned by Elias Jackson "Lucky" Baldwin who made a fortune in Comstock Lode stock and California real estate. Or they might've picked another popular resort, the Brockway Hotel, which boasted hot springs at the northern edge of the lake.

At about the same time, National Forests were established in the Tahoe basin, first as a reaction against the destructive timbering practices of the 19th century, later as a way of preserving scenic attractions and, finally, to protect the basin's environment.

Several attempts were made to convert the basin, or parts of it, into a National Park. They all failed. Partly, it was the cost; perhaps $250,000 in 1900 and several million in the mid-thirties. And partly, it was because logging had scarred the scenery and National Park inspectors didn't know how well the forests would restore themselves.

The period between 1900 and World War II is fondly known as "Old Tahoe" by those who remember it and by those who can only imagine it. It was the period of family resorts, like Meeks Bay, Richardson's, and May-Ah-Mee; elegant resorts like Tahoe Tavern and Brockway Hot Springs; and large lakeshore estates.

Some of the wealthier citizens of the San Francisco Bay Area enjoyed their summers at Tahoe's resorts so much, they built their own summer mansions along the western lakeshore.

A few of these historic estates are still standing and available to the public. The Pope estate with its polo field, and Valhalla with its great hall, are just west of Camp Richardson; they now belong to the U.S. Forest Service. The 1,200-acre Ehrman Estate with its granite and shingle three-story lodge, two boat houses, children's house, and power plant is near Tahoma; it's now Sugar Pine Point State Park. Scandinavian royalty could have lived in three-story, granite and timbered Vikingsholm with its wildflower dappled sod roof; it's now the sole estate on Emerald Bay and part of the California State Park system.

Rustic Drum estate on the west shore and Whittell's "castle" on the east shore are privately owned. The famous Kaiser estate, Fleur du Lac, near Homewood, has been converted into luxurious condominiums, but the old stone boathouse and harbor remain. Lakeshore estates, large and small, new and old, still dot the shoreline, but the relaxed, rustic, elegant life of bygone Tahoe summers are only dim memories.

After World War II, the character of the Tahoe basin changed. Some say it was the 1960 Olympics at Squaw Valley, some blame it on the South Shore casinos, others accept it as another manifestation of post-war lifestyles.

Highways to and around the lake brought hordes of tourists and traffic congestion. Roadhouse casinos on the Nevada side of the lake sprouted into glittering highrises. Ropetows and ungroomed slopes blossomed into world-class ski resorts. And after World War II and Korean War veterans got themselves settled into the suburbs, they started looking for mountain retreats.

THE NEED TO GET AWAY AND RELAX HAS LED MANY PEOPLE TO TAHOE.

Soon bulldozers were transforming forest and marshes into subdivisions. Construction vied with tourism to become Tahoe's principal industry. As each new wave of part-time residents and tourists invaded the basin, the previous wave complained about congestion and urbanization caused by the newcomers.

Then, in the 1960s, scientists found that the lake's fabled clarity was slowly being degraded, and that the lake's population of algae was expanding. The blame was laid on sewage effluent, septic tanks, and soil disturbances on the hillsides. Atmospheric pollutants blown in from agricultural and metropolitan areas to the west were also suspected.

Nevada and California tried to solve Tahoe's growth problems by forming regional planning groups, but the control of a basin shared by two states and five counties was too much for them. In 1969, the governors of California and Nevada, Ronald Reagan and Paul Laxalt, agreed to a bistate compact, which was then ratified by the United States Congress. The compact called for a single planning agency for the entire basin.

Septic tanks were banned and sewage effluents were piped out of the basin. Dumps were closed. Building requirements were tightened. New subdivisions were discouraged.

But traffic congestion increased. The building of homes, motels, and casinos continued. Old resorts disappeared under condominium developments. The lake's clarity continued to decline.

Lawsuits were filed by land owners and by environmental groups. The Tahoe Regional Planning Agency was in disarray.

In 1980, both states negotiated a new compact that resulted in a stronger Tahoe Regional Planning Agency. The compact called for the agency to determine the environmental carrying capacity of the Tahoe basin and to develop a plan to guarantee that this capacity would not be exceeded.

A new regional plan was prepared, but environmental groups and California's Attorney General charged that it wouldn't adequately protect the basin. They filed a lawsuit barring implementation of the plan.

In an effort toward conciliation, consensus workshops were formed with all parties that had an interest in the basin. They included public agencies, environmentalists, property owners and local businesses.

In 1987, a new, restrictive regional plan was adopted; however, objections persist and constitutional questions continue to be tested in court.

Public agencies are buying land in order to prevent further development of streamzones, wetlands and steep parcels with fragile soils. Wildlife habitats and wetlands are being restored. Public agencies are also purchasing additional public access to the lake. More than 80 percent of the basin's lands are now owned by the public.

Standing on the slopes of Tahoe's watershed and looking at the spectacular scenery, or cruising on the lake and seeing the still fabulous clarity of the water, inspires a faith in the future of Tahoe. A new awareness of environmental issues has emerged from the struggles between property owner and environmental groups. New community plans sensitive to the beauty and ecology of the basin promise to assure quality development.

Additional research data and new interpretations will undoubtedly result in a better understanding of the lake's ecology and how to live with it. This book reminds us all of the beautiful natural features of the Tahoe basin, why we love it and why we need to care for it.

THE PROFILE OF A DEAD
PINE AGAINST AN EVENING
SKY. LEFT: A PINE NEEDLE
FLOATS ON THE SURFACE
OF LAKE TAHOE.

Spring

THE SNOWY COLD OF
WINTER LIES IN THE PAST.
A FLOWER AND BEETLE
SHARE IN THE WARMTH
OF THE SPRING SUN.

DUE TO THEIR ABRASIVE
NATURE AND BEAUTY,
STELLAR JAYS ARE OFTEN
HATED AS MUCH AS
THEY ARE LOVED. LEFT:
MOISTURE-LADEN
CLOUDS FLOAT ABOVE
DOLLAR POINT.

WATER FROM MELTING
SNOWS CASCADES DOWN
EAGLE FALLS HIGH ABOVE
EMERALD BAY.

CALICO FLOWERS COME TO
LIFE IN A DAMP MOUNTAIN
MEADOW NEAR MT. ROSE.
LEFT: SUN, WATER AND
GRASS JOIN TOGETHER AT
THE BEGINNING OF THE
MIDDLE FORK OF THE
AMERICAN RIVER.

A LONE HOT-AIR BALLOON
OFFERS THE BEST SEAT
IN THE HOUSE FOR THE
SUNRISE SHOW.

AFTER THE SKI RESORTS
CLOSE AND THE
SNOWPACK BEGINS TO
SHRINK, THE BACK-
COUNTRY SKIER REJOICES
IN BEAUTIFUL SUNRISES
AND SMOOTH CORN
SNOW. RIGHT: LINGERING
SNOW GROWS WRINKLED
WITH AGE AS THE SUN
FINISHES ANOTHER DAY'S
SHINING ON MT. TALLAC.

A Columbine finds its home growing amongst the lush surroundings of Shirley Canyon. Left: An aspen grove on the west shore bursts with green life.

Ponderosa pines reach
up from the water's
edge on the east shore.
Right: Looking down
on Crystal Bay from
Marlette Peak.

WALKING ALONG THE
ROAD FROM SPOONER
SUMMIT TO MARLETTE
LAKE IS ALWAYS A SCENIC
PLEASURE. IN SPRING,
WILDFLOWERS ABOUND
IN WONDERFUL VARIETY.
RIGHT: A BLADE OF
GRASS AFTER AN
EVENING RAIN SHOWER.

Nothing is more astounding than a nearby lightning strike accompanied by booming thunder. Left: A late afternoon thunder shower above Stateline begins to clear, leaving a rainbow in its wake.

SURFING A WAVE ON THE
SOUTH FORK OF THE YUBA
RIVER. IN THE SPRING,
RIVERS SWELL IN SIZE TO
THE DELIGHT OF KAYAKERS.

Hiking the Pacific Crest
Trail between Squaw
Valley and Sugar Bowl
has become a spring-
time ritual for
wildflower lovers.
Right: Spring run-off
creates large volumes
of water that seem to
leap into the air.

The sun is warm and the water may look "tropical" but a dip of the toes reminds us that it's a long way from the South Pacific. Right: Crystal clear water reflects the brilliant sky above.

Summer

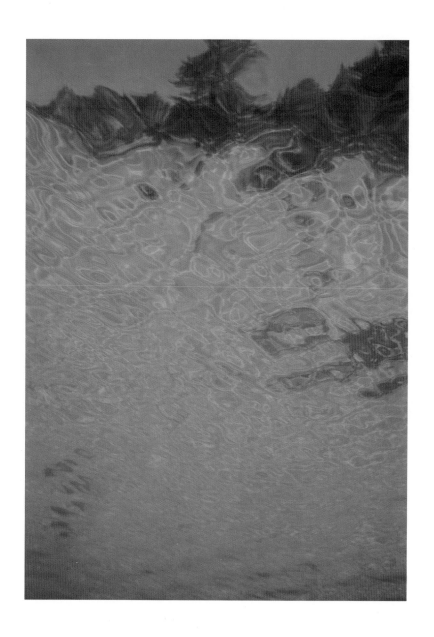

A TROUT'S-EYE VIEW OF
A RIPPLED SHORELINE
REFLECTED IN THE
SURFACE.

Summer is the time to immerse yourself in an underwater world of cold, blue-green beauty. Left: After a quick-paced ascent of Pyramid Peak, a tired hiker finds relief from the sun in the waters of Lake Aloha.

TAHOE MAKES A PERFECT
HOME FOR PRACTITIONERS
IN THE FINE ART OF
RECREATION. RIGHT:
SAILING ON AIR HIGH
ABOVE THE WAVES OF
LAKE TAHOE.

In one of the most
exposed sports, a wind-
surfer thrives on high
winds and large waves.
Left: The leader of the
annual Trans-Tahoe
race pulls away from
the rest of the pack.

THE SMALL TEA HOUSE
PERCHED ON EMERALD
ISLE MAKES THE SPACIOUS
ESTATE OF VIKINGSHOLM
EVEN MORE ENCHANTING.
RIGHT: YEAR 'ROUND
RESIDENTS OF LAKE
TAHOE, A MERGANSER
FAMILY PASSES THE WEST
SHORE IN PURSUIT OF AN
UNDERWATER MEAL.

A FEW PATCHES OF SNOW
ON DICKS PEAK ARE ALL
THAT REMAIN OF THE PAST
WINTER.

DEPENDING ON ONE'S ATTITUDE, CARRYING A HEAVY PACK INTO THE WILDERNESS CAN BE EITHER A BURDEN OR AN UPLIFT- ING JOY. LEFT: CAMPING UNDER THE PATHS OF STARS REVEALS ANOTHER EXAMPLE OF NATURE'S CIRCULAR RHYTHMS.

A DEAD PINE STANDS
SILHOUETTED AGAINST THE
LAST RAYS OF SUN
STRIKING TAHOE'S
SURFACE. RIGHT: A RISING
SUN PEAKS THROUGH
ROCKS ATOP ELLIS PEAK.

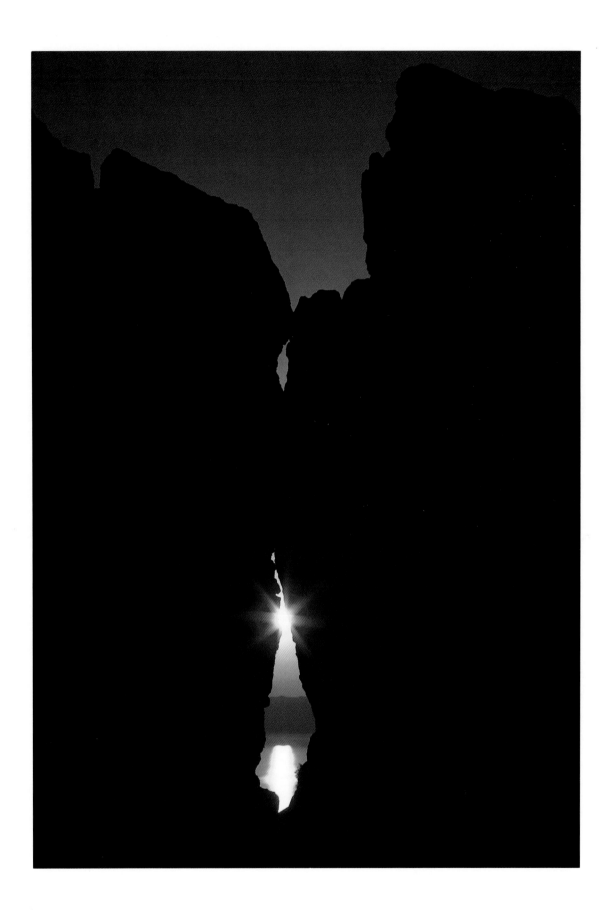

Most people never
forget the first time
they enter Emerald Bay
by boat. Right: Boaters
headed toward
Chimney Beach seem to
be riding a "magic
boat" as it seemingly
levitates on the surface.

OFTEN FED AND SELDOM
HUNTED, THE GEESE OF
TAHOE HAVE DEVELOPED A
FAIRLY PEACEFUL COEXIS-
TENCE WITH MAN. LEFT: A
GNARLED JUNIPER TREE
REFLECTS A HARSH LIFE ON
THE EASTERN SHORELINE.

THE SURROUNDING
FOREST IS MIRRORED IN
THE SMALLEST OF THE
FIVE LAKES.

THE BRILLIANT GREEN OF
SUMMER GROWS MORE
INTENSE ON THE DAMP
SLOPES FAVORED BY A
WIDE VARIETY OF PLANT
LIFE. RIGHT: MARLETTE
LAKE REMAINS A SANC-
TUARY FOR CUTTHROAT
TROUT WHICH ONCE
THRIVED IN LAKE TAHOE.

For some, simply
wiggling their toes in
the sand is the high-
light of the day. Left:
As Taylor Creek enters
the lake, it forms one
of the largest stretches
of sand beach in Tahoe.

ANOTHER WARM SUMMER
DAY FADES INTO THE QUIET
CALM OF A WEST SHORE
SUNSET.

Often photographed from the outside, the tea house window on Emerald Isle offers another view. Right: At one time, a bridge was planned across the entrance to Emerald Bay. Fortunately, public outcry killed the idea.

THE NATIVE WASHO
INDIANS BELIEVED LAKE
TAHOE WAS INHABITED BY
POWERFUL SPIRITS LIVING
IN ITS WATERS. A FULL
MOON SETTING OVER THE
WEST SHORE ADDS TO ITS
MAGIC. LEFT: LENTICULAR
CLOUDS OVER MT. ROSE
ARE SIGNS THAT A CHANGE
IN WEATHER IS NEAR.

Autumn

WITH THE APPROACH OF
WINTER, LEAVES YELLOW
AND FALL TO THE GROUND
SOON COVERED BY
MORNING FROST.

Aspen-filled canyons reveal some history of past sheepherders and explorers who left their marks on the white bark. Left: Groves of quaking aspens such as these at Marlette Lake leave little doubt of winter's coming.

A "FISH-EYE" VIEW OF FALL
COLORS NEAR SPOONER
SUMMIT. RIGHT: AS THE
BREEZE BLOWS, THE ASPENS
DANCE WITH COLORED
MOTION.

THE SUMMERTIME CROWDS
HAVE GONE AND A DUST-
ING OF SNOW COVERS THE
PEAKS. TIME TO CONTEM-
PLATE THE PAST DAYS OF
SUMMER AND THE
APPROACH OF WINTER.

THE SUN RISES ABOVE
STATELINE POINT BRINGING
WARMTH TO A FROSTY
BEACH. RIGHT: AS WINTER
APPROACHES, HOPEFUL
SAILORS LEAVE THEIR BOATS
IN THE WATER IN
ANTICIPATION OF "JUST
ONE MORE DAY" OF
SAILING ON THE LAKE.

TRUSTING FRIENDS SHARE
IN THE PLEASURE OF
CLIMBING EAGLE LAKE
BUTTRESS. RIGHT: WITH A
MOUNTAIN BIKE COME THE
BENEFITS OF UPHILL
EXERCISE AND THE THRILLS
OF DOWNHILL SPEED.

A COLORFUL BROOK
TROUT WELL-FATTENED IN
PREPARATION FOR A LONG
WINTER'S STAY BENEATH
THE ICE OF A BACK-
COUNTRY LAKE. LEFT:
WHILE FISHING IS AN
ENJOYABLE PURSUIT IN
ITSELF, JUST BEING IN A
BEAUTIFUL SPOT AT
SUNRISE CAN BE AS
REWARDING AS LANDING
A TROUT.

A COLT PEERS OUT FROM
BEHIND ITS MOTHER ON A
COLD FROSTY MORNING IN
SQUAW VALLEY. THE
VALLEY'S NAME COMES
FROM A TIME WHEN
SETTLERS PASSED
THROUGH AND OBSERVED
INDIAN WOMEN AND
CHILDREN AWAITING THE
RETURN OF THEIR
HUNTERS.

Water grasses grow in the calm shelter of Emerald Bay's entrance. Right: A pair of herons pause in their search for food along Baldwin Beach. The Taylor Creek-Baldwin Beach area is some of the last prime undeveloped wetlands in the Tahoe basin.

Sunshine begins to fade
on a deserted beach
near Vikingsholm.
Empty picnic tables are
a reminder of warm
summer days — now
just a memory.

Frost-covered mule ears leaves on Martis Peak. Right: A colorful grove of brilliant aspens on the shores of Emerald Bay.

EMERALD ISLE SUR-
ROUNDED BY THE COLORS
OF THE EARLY MORNING
SKY REFLECTED IN
EMERALD BAY. LEFT:
BEFORE THE COMING OF
THE WHITE MAN, THE
WASHO INDIANS LIVED IN
HARMONY WITH NATURE
AND ACCEPTED TAHOE'S
SEASONAL OFFERINGS OF
AN ABUNDANCE OF FISH.

AN APPROACHING STORM
ROUGHENS THE WATER
SURROUNDING A
HOMEWARD-BOUND
CANOEIST. LEFT: AN
INVERSION OF CLOUDS
MEETS THE SUN AND A
TREE ON EAGLE ROCK.

Winter

THE LAST GLOW OF SUN
FADES INTO A LONG, COLD
WINTER NIGHT.

A PARTING STORM REVEALS A BRIGHT, MORNING SUN. RIGHT: AN INVERSION OF CLOUDS HANGS ABOVE THE LAKE, RUMORED TO HIDE A LARGE UNIDENTIFIED CREATURE LIVING IN ITS DEEP, DARK WATERS.

ALL THE ELEMENTS OF
WINTER AT TAHOE — SUN
AND CLOUDS, WATER AND
SNOW.

The shared dream of many skiers . . . wallowing in deep powder snow. Left: Getting off the beaten path has its rewards.

PUSHING THE LIMITS AT
ALPINE MEADOWS.
LEFT: SHOWING SOME
COURAGE AT SLIDE
MOUNTAIN.

WITH MANY SUNSETS IN
ITS PAST, SUGAR BOWL
HAS A LONG, COLORFUL
HISTORY OF SKIING.
LEFT: DAYS LIKE THESE
KEEP SKIERS COMING BACK
TO THE MOUNTAINS
AROUND TAHOE.

A full moon over
Desolation Wilderness
viewed from atop Mt.
Tallac.

EMERALD ISLE DRESSED IN
A COAT OF WINTER WHITE.
LEFT: A HIGHFLYING
EYEFUL OF LAKE TAHOE
BLUE.

Just when you think
you shouldn't be out
in the cold, the sparkle
of suspended ice
crystals warms you
inside. Right: Storm
clouds clear, leaving
behind a fresh dusting
of snow on the peaks
above the west shore.

BESIDES GETTING YOU UP
THE HILL, CHAIRLIFTS
PROVIDE A CHANCE TO
GATHER YOUR THOUGHTS
BETWEEN RUNS. LEFT:
SQUAW VALLEY ON THIS
WINTER DAY STARTS SKIERS'
HEARTS POUNDING IN
ANTICIPATION.

A young speedster experiences the slippery pleasures of snow. Left: When skiing the back country, it's quality, not quantity, that counts.

ADRENALIN PERMEATES
THE AIR AT THE START OF
THE GOLD RUSH RACE AT
ROYAL GORGE.

A BOATHOUSE ON THE
WEST SHORE IS DRAPED IN
A CURTAIN OF ICE. LEFT:
WHILE MANY PEOPLE ARE
STILL ASLEEP, OTHERS FIND
ANOTHER REWARDING WAY
TO START THE DAY.

Graceful expression is displayed in the beauty of ice skating. Right: Mt. Tallac in its winter splendor awaits the coming of another storm.

A BURST OF EARLY
MORNING SUNSHINE
FILTERS THROUGH AN
ASPEN GROVE. RIGHT:
BAREFOOT WALKS ALONG
THE BEACH ARE STILL
MANY MONTHS AWAY.

WATER ROUGHENED BY
WINDS FROM THE EAST
CAUSES ICE TO FORM
BENEATH THE PIERS.

YES, IT'S A REAL PHOTO-
GRAPH, AND NO, THERE
ISN'T A SKI RESORT AT
EMERALD BAY. LEFT:
LINGERING STORM CLOUDS
CLING TO THE WESTERN
RANGE FAR ACROSS THE
LAKE.

I DARE YOU TO RUN OFF
THE END OF THE PIER AND
DIVE IN! RIGHT: A FARE-
WELL SIGHT TO MANY
VISITORS OF THE TAHOE
AREA, DONNER LAKE LIES
IN THE GRIP OF WINTER'S
HAND.